KINGS AND QUEENS

ARC

BOUDICA

EDWARD THE CONFESSOR

WILLIAM THE CONQUEROR

JONES

WREN

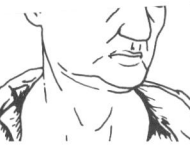

HAWKSMOOR

RICHARD I

EDWARD I

HENRY V

VANBRUGH

ADAM

NASH

HENRY VII

HENRY VIII

ELIZABETH I

SOANE

SCOTT

SHAW

JAMES VI AND I

CHARLES I

CHARLES II

VOYSEY

MACKINTOSH

LUTYENS

GEORGE III

VICTORIA

ELIZABETH II

DREW

STIRLING

FOSTER

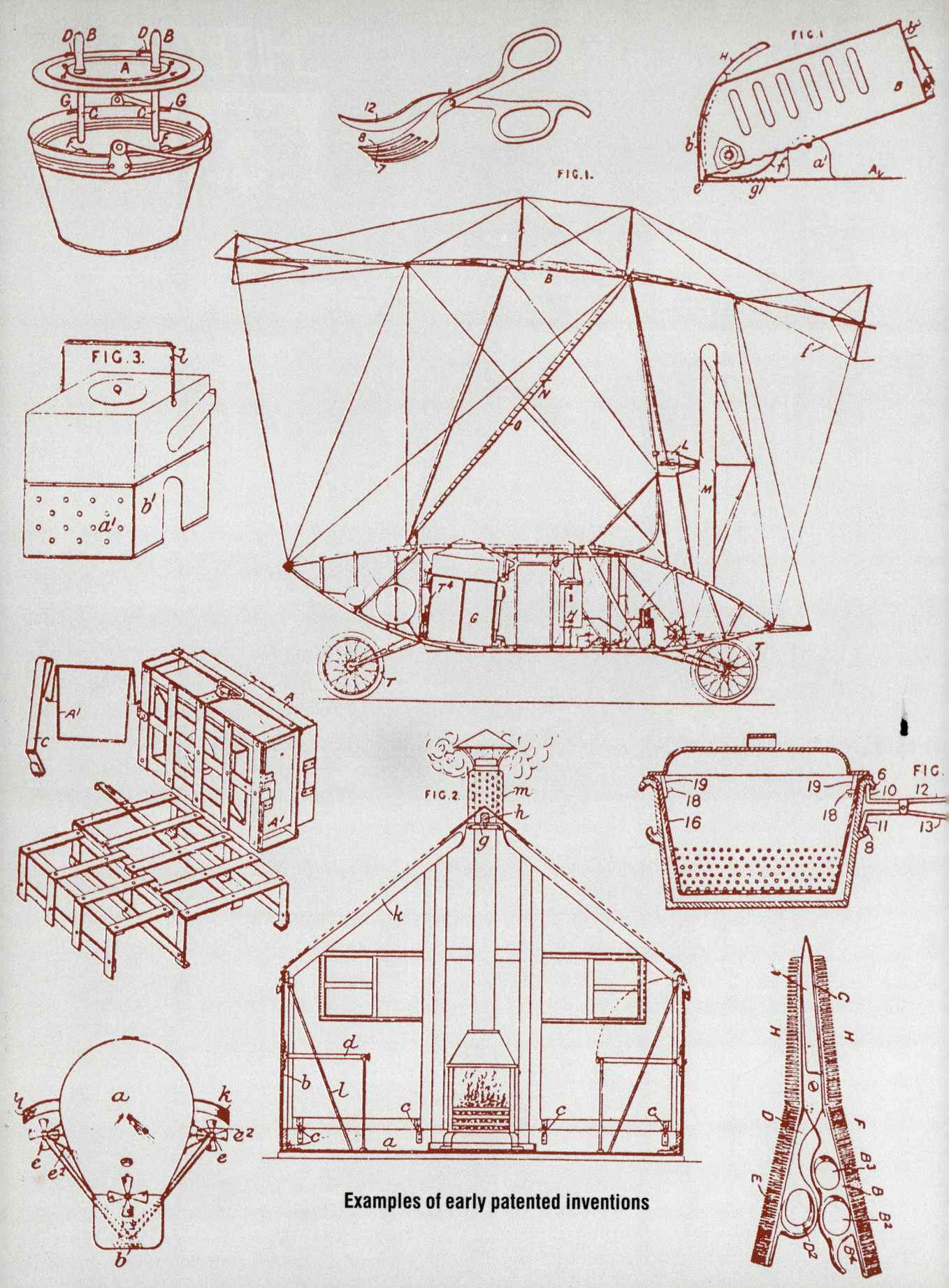

Examples of early patented inventions

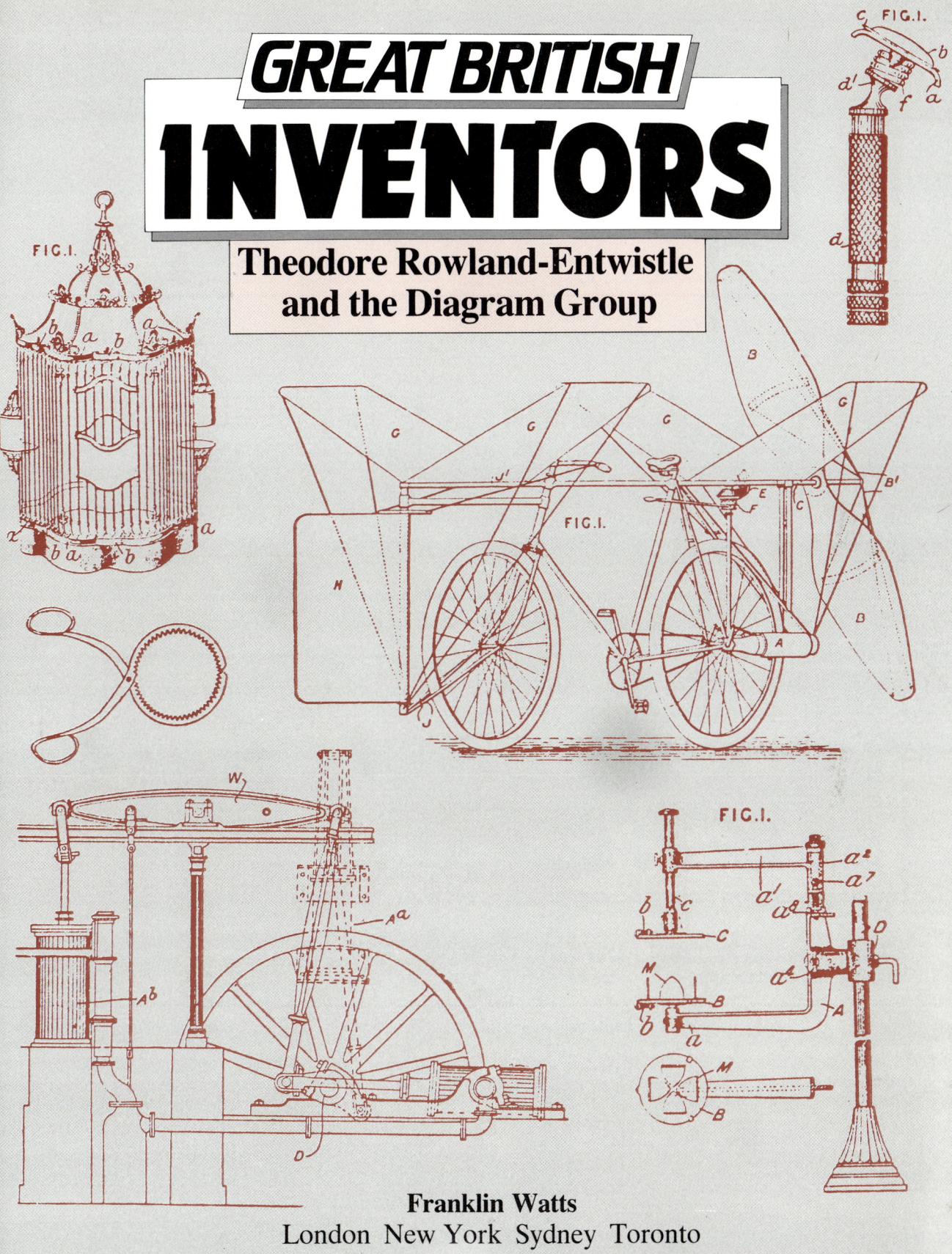

GREAT BRITISH
INVENTORS

Theodore Rowland-Entwistle
and the Diagram Group

Franklin Watts

London New York Sydney Toronto

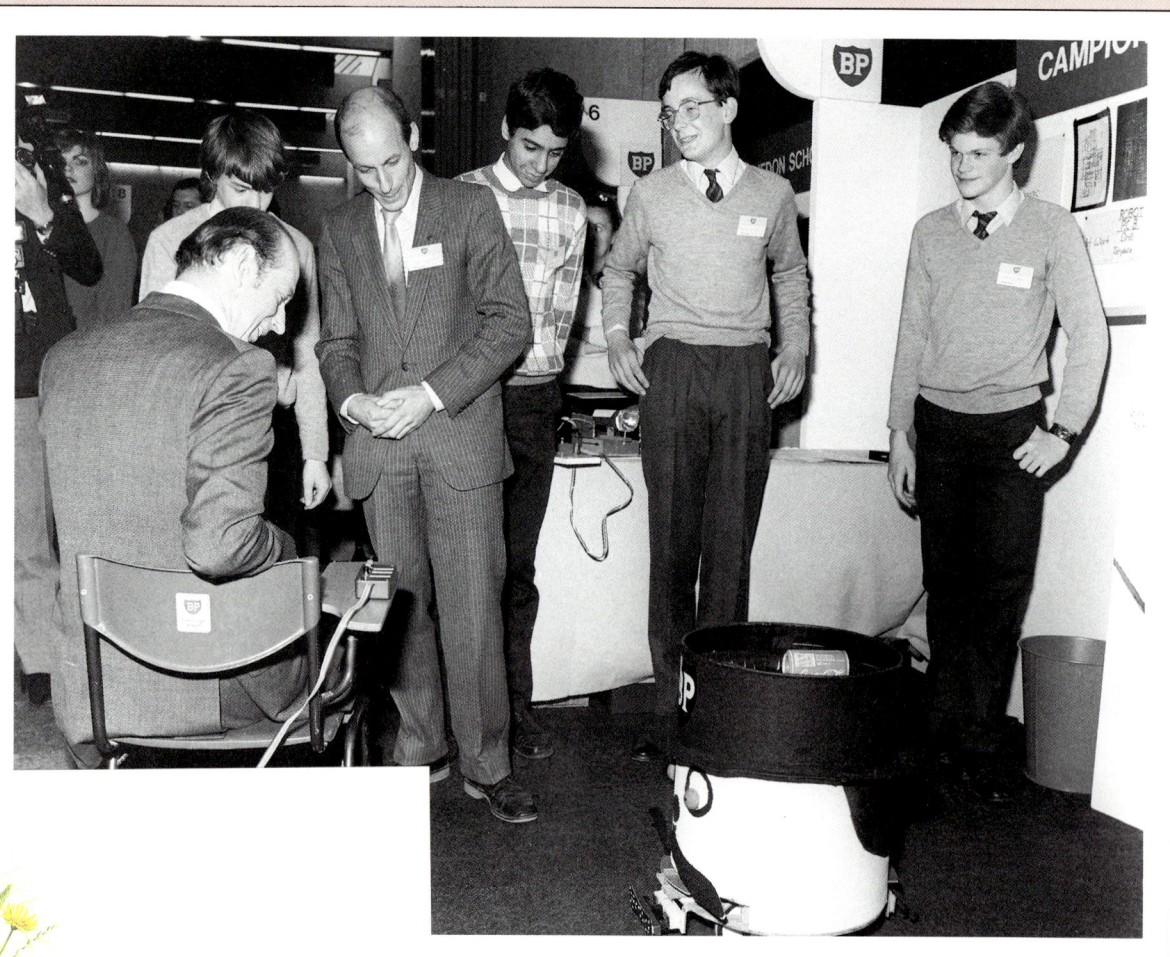

wledgements
e research: IKON
BP Oil Ltd
ulton Picture Library: 28, 34
Ltd: 2
ndustries Ltd: 22, 23
20
ll Collection: 8, 12, 16, 18, 22, 24
34
ting Roadstuds Ltd: 30
onan Picture Library: 15, 25
Airforce Museum: 35
ire Post: 31

This book belongs to :

VANESSA PRYCE

Contents

© Diagram Visual Information Ltd 1986

First published in Great Britain 1986 by
Franklin Watts Ltd
12a Golden Square
London W1

Printed in Singapore

ISBN 0 86313 365 7

When they lived

1642–1651 English
Civil War

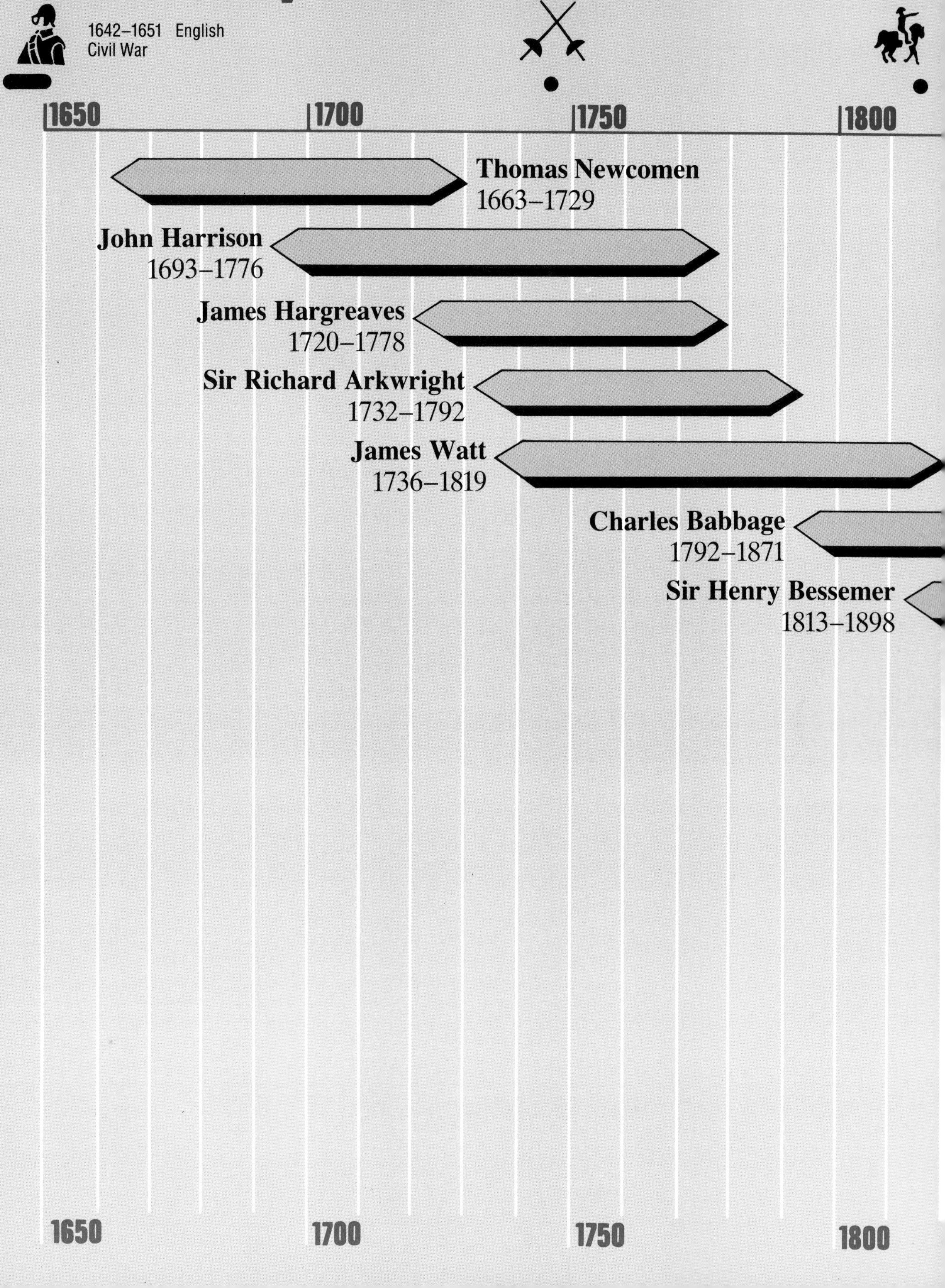

1746 Bonnie Prince
Charlie defeated at Culloden

1815 Battle
of Waterloo

|1650 |1700 |1750 |1800

Thomas Newcomen
1663–1729

John Harrison
1693–1776

James Hargreaves
1720–1778

Sir Richard Arkwright
1732–1792

James Watt
1736–1819

Charles Babbage
1792–1871

Sir Henry Bessemer
1813–1898

1650   1700   1750   1800

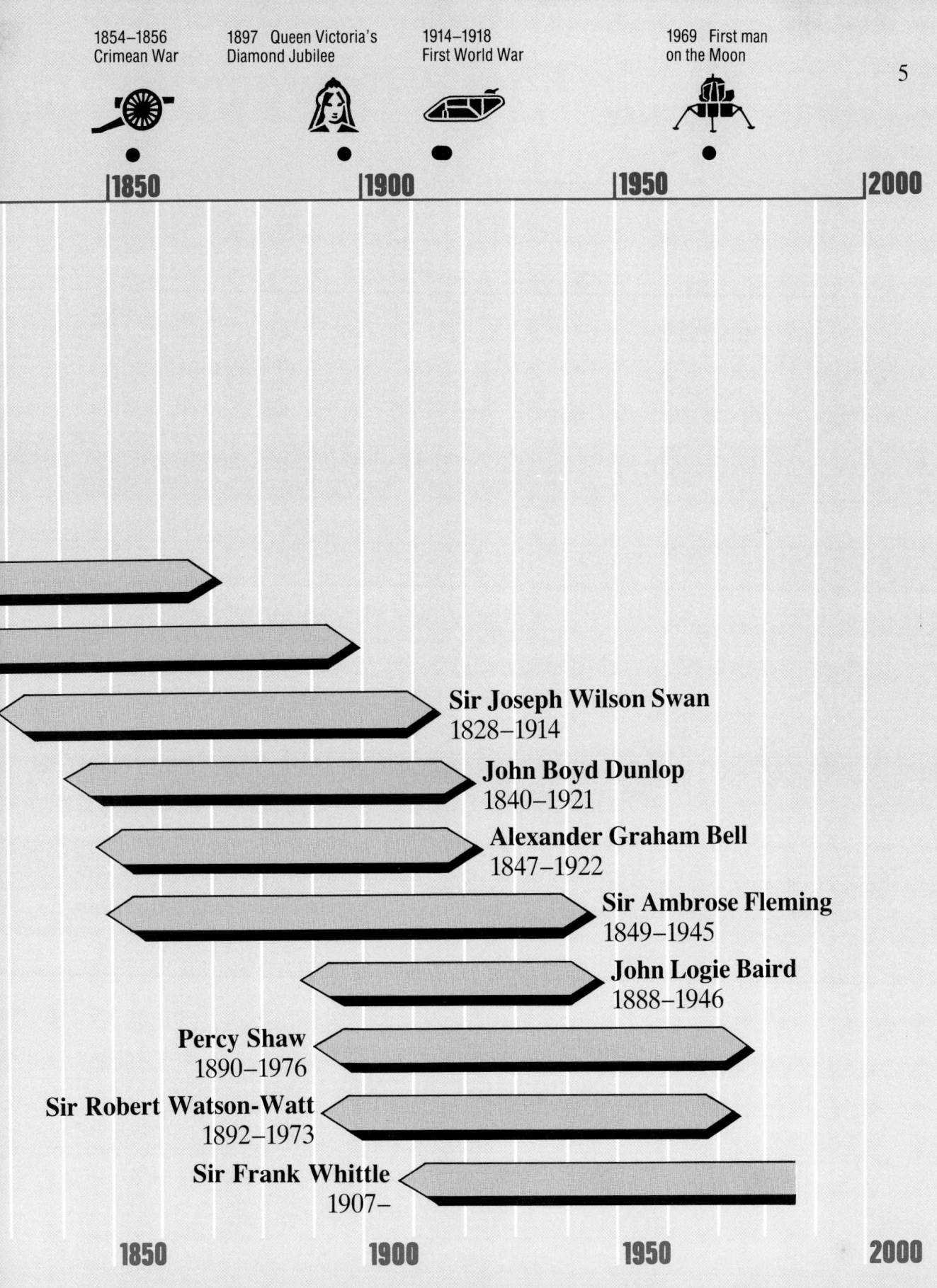

1854–1856 Crimean War

1897 Queen Victoria's Diamond Jubilee

1914–1918 First World War

1969 First man on the Moon

5

1850　1900　1950　2000

Sir Joseph Wilson Swan
1828–1914

John Boyd Dunlop
1840–1921

Alexander Graham Bell
1847–1922

Sir Ambrose Fleming
1849–1945

John Logie Baird
1888–1946

Percy Shaw
1890–1976

Sir Robert Watson-Watt
1892–1973

Sir Frank Whittle
1907–

1850　1900　1950　2000

Thomas Newcomen

Thomas Newcomen was one of the first people to make a successful steam engine, which was used as a pump for removing water from mines. We know very little about his life, except that he was born in Dartmouth into a moderately prosperous Baptist family, was married and had two sons. He was trained as a metalworker and toolsmith, and was in business in Dartmouth.

Newcomen lived in an area of tin mines which were notorious for flooding. Newcomen heard of experiments by a French-born engineer, Denis Papin, then working in England, to condense steam to create a vacuum and raise water. So he began experiments along the same lines, helped by a glazier and plumber, John Calley.

Meanwhile Captain Thomas Savery, a military engineer, had constructed a primitive steam pump. Savery's steam-pump was not powerful enough to work in mines, while Newcomen's was. So the two men went into partnership.

The first working Newcomen engine was installed at a coal mine at Dudley, Staffordshire, in 1712. It could lift 46 litres (10 gallons) of water a distance of 47 metres (153 feet) at each stroke of its huge piston, which made 12 strokes a minute.

The Newcomen engine played an important part in the Industrial Revolution of the 1700s. With its aid tin and coal mines that had become unworkable because of flooding could be reopened. It was also reliable, even if it was clumsy and relatively inefficient. A few Newcomen engines remained in operation until the early 1900s, though they had been modified in the light of later inventions. Newcomen continued to build and install pumping engines until his death.

1663
Born in February in Dartmouth, Devon
1705
Married Hannah Waymouth; with John Calley completed 'machine for raising water by fire'
1712
Newcomen steam engine installed at coal mine near Dudley Castle
1717
Calley died in Whitworth, near Leeds
1729
Newcomen died 5th August in London

The Newcomen Memorial Engine

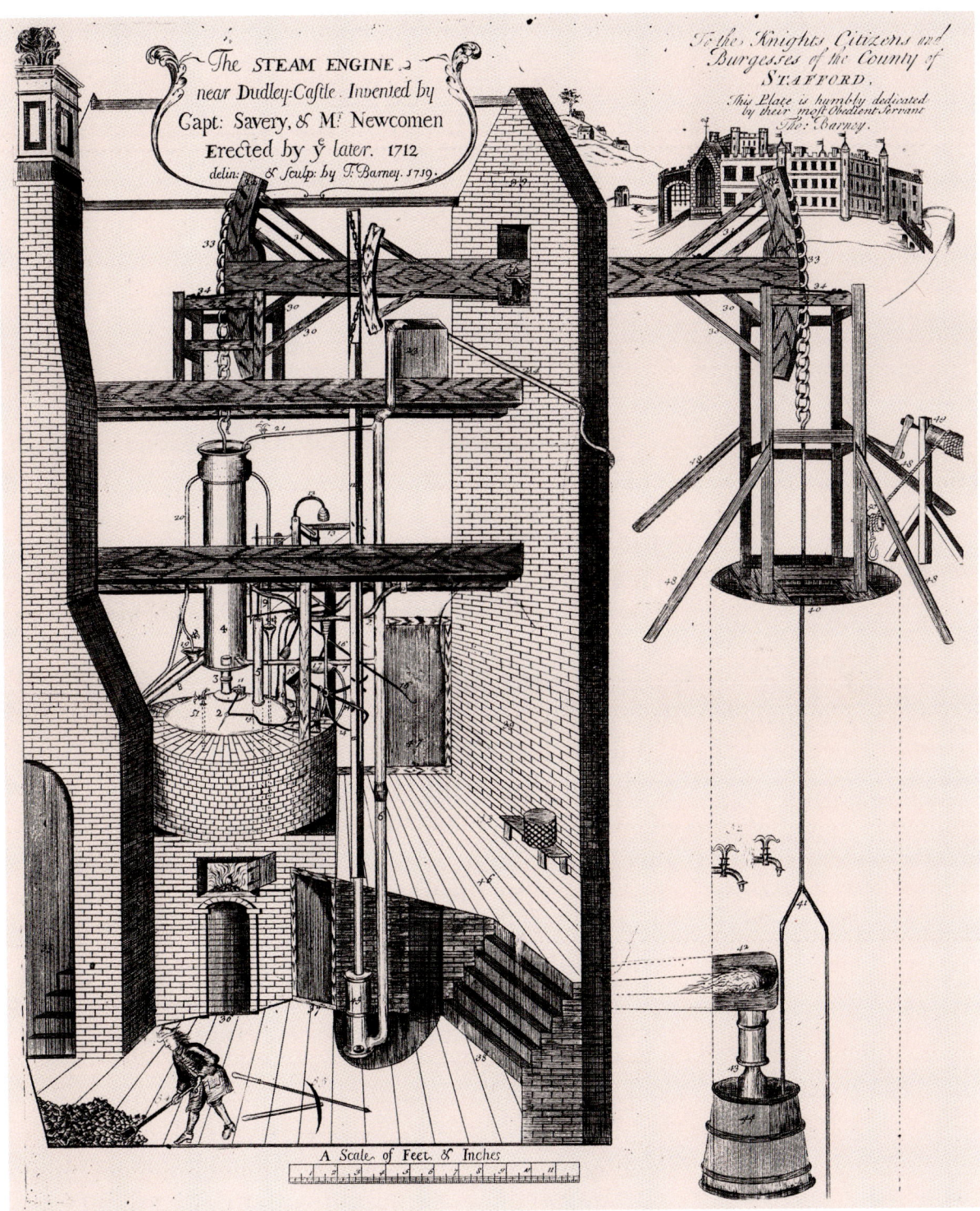

John Harrison

Witnesses to Harrison's ability to construct accurate timepieces

John Harrison invented the first accurate marine chronometer (clock), which greatly improved navigation at sea. Harrison was born in Foulby, near Pontefract, Yorkshire, in 1693. He was the son of a carpenter. When he was seven years old his family moved to Barrow-on-Humber, Lincolnshire, where Harrison lived for 36 years before he moved to London.

As soon as Harrison was old enough he joined his father in the carpentry trade. However, he was fascinated by machinery, and especially by clocks and watches, and although he had little formal schooling, he taught himself the elements of mechanics. When he was 22 he combined his trade and his hobby and made an eight-day clock mechanism entirely of wood.

In 1713 a government body, the Board of Longitude, offered a prize of £20,000 to anyone who could invent a method of calculating a ship's longitude (its position east-west) to within 48 km

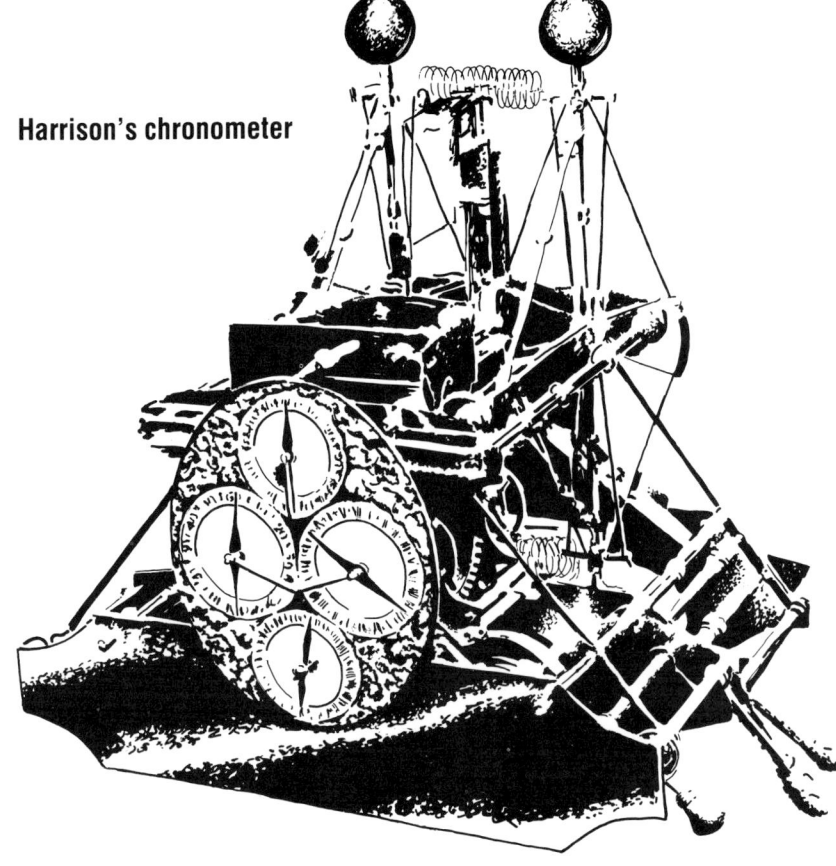

Harrison's chronometer

A long-case clock by James and John Harrison

(30 miles). Sailors could calculate latitude (its position north-south) just by observations of the sun and stars, but for longitude they needed an accurate clock.

Harrison was determined to win the prize. It took him seven years to build his first marine chronometer. To test it he was sent in a Royal Navy ship on a voyage to Lisbon and back, and was awarded £500. He proceeded to make three more chronometers, each smaller and more accurate than the last. Harrison's son William tested the fourth chronometer on a voyage to Jamaica and back, and found it could be used to calculate longitude to within 29 km (18 miles).

The Board of Longitude's recognition of Harrison's success was grudging, and it recommended paying only half the prize money. Finally in 1773 King George III intervened, and Harrison received the rest.

James Hargreaves

Spinning linen in an Irish cottage

1720
Born in Oswaldtwistle, Lancashire
1760
Invented an improved carding machine for combing cotton fibres
1764
Invented the spinning jenny
1768
Home and machines smashed by mob; set up cotton mill in Nottingham
1770
Failed to patent the spinning jenny
1778
Died 22nd April in Nottingham

James Hargreaves was one of the pioneers of the Industrial Revolution. His invention of the spinning jenny enabled one person to do the work of eight.

Hargreaves was born in Oswaldtwistle, near Blackburn, Lancashire, in 1720. He worked as a carpenter. At that time spinning thread and weaving it into cloth was something people did at home in their cottages. The woman of the household spun the thread during the day, and in the evening the man of the house wove the thread into cloth on a handloom. Hargreaves and his family made cloth in this way.

In 1733 another Lancashire man, James Kay, had invented a flying shuttle, which doubled the speed at which cloth could be woven. By 1760 its use was widespread, and the weavers were working faster than the spinners could produce thread. One day Hargreaves' daughter Jenny knocked her spinning wheel over. As it lay on its side Hargreaves realised that he could make a

machine with several horizontal spindles, and so produce thread faster.

The spinning jenny

Hargreaves built a frame with a row of eight spindles which could be turned by one wheel with a handle. He called it a 'spinning jenny' after his daughter. As long as he had just the one machine in his own home there was no trouble, but when he sold several machines to friends, the other spinners and weavers in the villages around Blackburn rioted. They feared the new technology would put them out of their jobs. An angry mob marched to Hargreaves' home and smashed it up, with his machines. He and his family had to flee to Nottingham.

There, Hargreaves found a business partner, Thomas James. The two men set up a cotton mill. James advised him to patent the spinning jenny, but Hargreaves could not do so because he had already sold several machines. Six years after Hargreaves died in 1768 there were 20,000 spinning jennies in use.

Sir Richard Arkwright

The water mill at Cromford, Derbyshire *(right)*

1732
Born 23rd December in Preston
1750
Started work as a barber and wig-maker in Bolton
1755
Married Patients Holt 31st March
1761
Married Margaret Biggins, 24th March
1768
Opened spinning mill in Nottingham
1769
Took out first patent
1771
Opened new water-powered mill in Cromford, Derbyshire
1773
Produced England's first all-cotton cloth

Richard Arkwright was a man of enormous energy, who worked from five in the morning until nine at night. This capacity for hard work enabled him to revolutionise cotton production and become a rich man.

Arkwright was born in Preston, Lancashire, in 1732, and was the youngest member of a large family. He had only a very elementary schooling, but he continued to educate himself until he was in his 50s.

At the age of 18 Arkwright set up in business as a barber and wig-maker in Bolton. While travelling around buying hair for wigs he met many cotton weavers, and noticed that they had to use linen for the warp threads, the ones running from end to end of the fabric. The spinning jenny invented by James Hargreaves did not produce a strong enough cotton thread for this purpose. So Arkwright set to work to design a new spinning frame. In it the cotton passed between rollers moving at different speeds, which made the thread

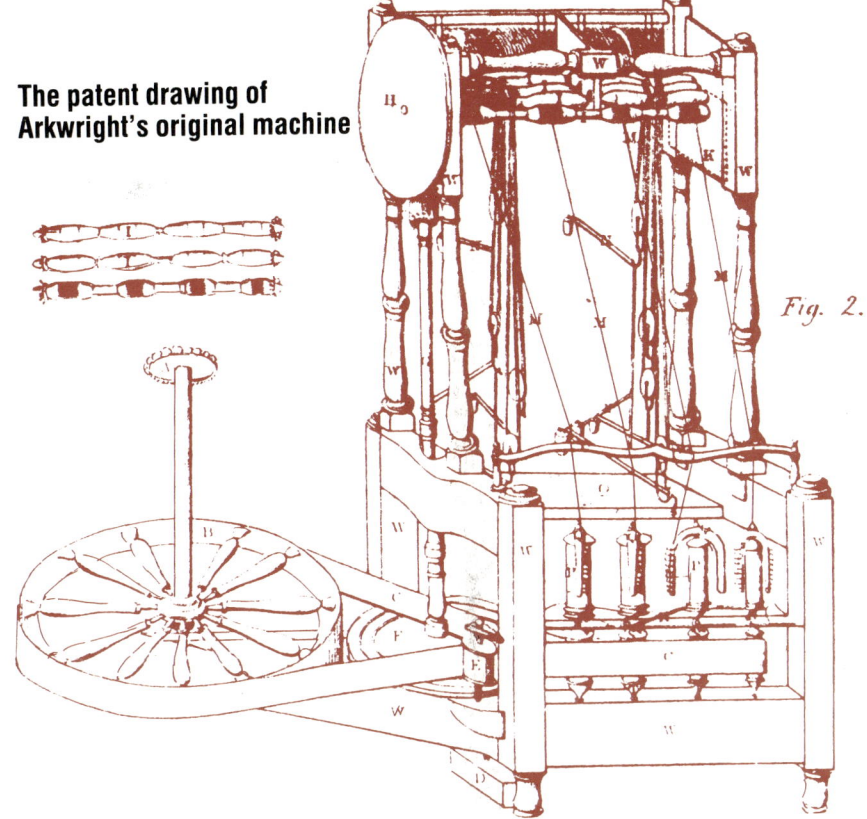

The patent drawing of Arkwright's original machine

Fig. 2.

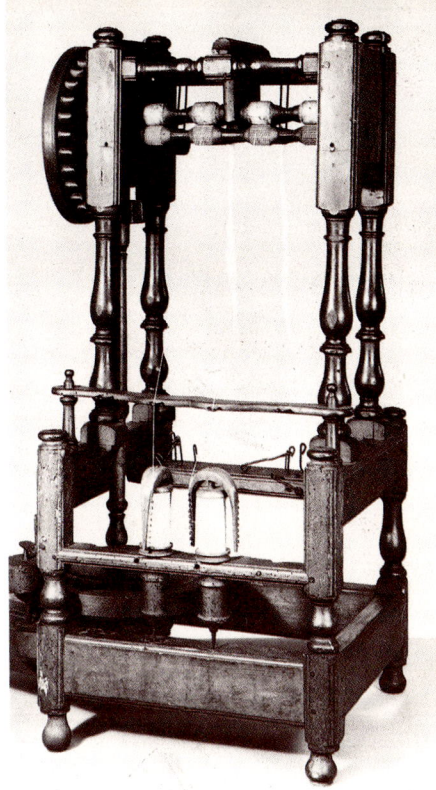

The original spinning machine

finer and stronger. A clockmaker helped him construct the machine.

Arkwright set up his first machine at a house in Preston, where the humming noise it made led local people to fear some form of witchcraft. So he moved to Nottingham and opened a spinning mill, with power supplied by horses. However, horsepower was not enough, so he set up a new factory at Cromford in Derbyshire, where a fast-flowing stream provided water-power. His machine became known as a 'water-frame'.

Arkwright took out two patents to try to safeguard his invention, but after a series of law-suits the courts decided he was not entitled to them. Another set-back was the destruction of a mill Arkwright built at Chorley, Lancashire, by workers who feared the new machines would take away their jobs. By this time, however, Arkwright was well established in business and was knighted when he was 54, and became High Sheriff of Derbyshire.

1775
Took out second patent
1779
Mob destroyed mill in Chorley, Lancashire
1781-1785
Engaged in lawsuits, lost his patents
1786
Received knighthood
1787
Appointed High Sheriff of Derbyshire
1790
Installed steam-power at a mill in Nottingham
1792
Died 3rd August in Cromford

James Watt

A rotative engine used in Soho, Birmingham *(right)*

James Watt was a Scottish engineer who turned the primitive steam engine of Thomas Newcomen into an efficient and reliable source of power. He was born in 1736 in Greenock, on Clydeside. His father was a prosperous merchant, builder and shipowner. Watt's schooling was interrupted by periodic migraine headaches, but he was a studious child.

At the age of 18 he spent a year in London studying the craft of making mathematical instruments, then set up a workshop at Glasgow University. He married his cousin, Margaret Miller.

One day the university's model of Newcomen's engine was brought to Watt to repair. He noticed how inefficient it was. The steam in its cylinder was condensed back into water by cooling the cylinder, which then had to heat up again for the next stroke of the piston. Watt arranged for the steam to pass into a separate condenser, leaving the cylinder hot. His engine was more powerful and used less fuel.

James Watt's garret workshop

Lack of money prevented Watt from developing his engine further. He sold a share in the invention to an engineer, John Roebuck, who was also unable to develop it. To make a living, Watt worked for eight years as a surveyor, helping to build canals. His wife died, leaving him with young children.

Then Roebuck died, and Watt went into partnership with Matthew Boulton, a businessman who had set up the Soho Engineering Works near Birmingham. The two men began building engines and selling them. Watt settled down in Birmingham, and remarried.

The first Watt engines were pumps, used for clearing water from mines. In 1781 he devised a way of turning the to-and-fro motion of the piston into rotary motion so that the engine could turn machinery. Within a few years, Watt engines were powering factories all over Britain, and he became a very rich man. Watt retired at the age of 64, but spent the rest of his long life experimenting and inventing.

1736
Born 19th January in Greenock
1755
Trained in London
1764
Married Margaret Miller
1765
Invented his steam engine
1766-1774
Worked as a surveyor
1773
Margaret died
1775
Formed partnership with Matthew Boulton
1776
Married Ann MacGregor
1781
Invented rotary engine
1800
Retired from business
1819
Died 25th August, near Birmingham

Charles Babbage

1792
Born 26th December in Teignmouth
1811-1814
Studied at Cambridge
1815
Moved to London
1816
Elected Fellow of the Royal Society
1820
Helped found Royal Astronomical Society
1822
Announced invention of 'Difference Engine'
1828
Travelled in Europe
1828-1839
Professor of Mathematics at Cambridge
1831
Helped to found the British Association
1842
Work on 'Difference Engine' abandoned
1864
Published autobiography
1871
Died 18th October in London

Charles Babbage was a mathematician who tried to build what would have been the world's first digital computer. He failed because the technology of his time was not adequate for the task.

Babbage was born in 1792 near Teignmouth in Devon, the son of a banker. He read mathematics at Cambridge University, and was elected a Fellow of the Royal Society at only 24. While he was still a student he hit on the idea of a machine, which he called a 'Difference Engine', to calculate numerical tables. In 1822 Babbage was given a grant by the government to pay for his research.

Babbage worked at the 'Difference Engine' for four years, then spent a year travelling in Europe. During this time he studied the work of continental factories, and wrote a book, *Economy of Machines and Manufactures.*

On his return he secured more money from the government, but each time he had a machine nearly complete he destroyed it because he had thought of some improvement. Eventually, when he had spent £17,000 of the government's money and about £6,000 of his own, the scheme was abandoned. The partly finished machine was used to calculate tables of logarithms from 1 to 108,000.

By this time Babbage was working on an entirely new machine, the 'Analytical Engine'. It was to be programmed by punched cards, which would control the mechanism. In his written description of it Babbage described methods of calculation very like those in modern computers, but he never completed it because he was refused further funds. Although Babbage did not gain recognition in his own time, he is now considered to be the pioneer of computer science.

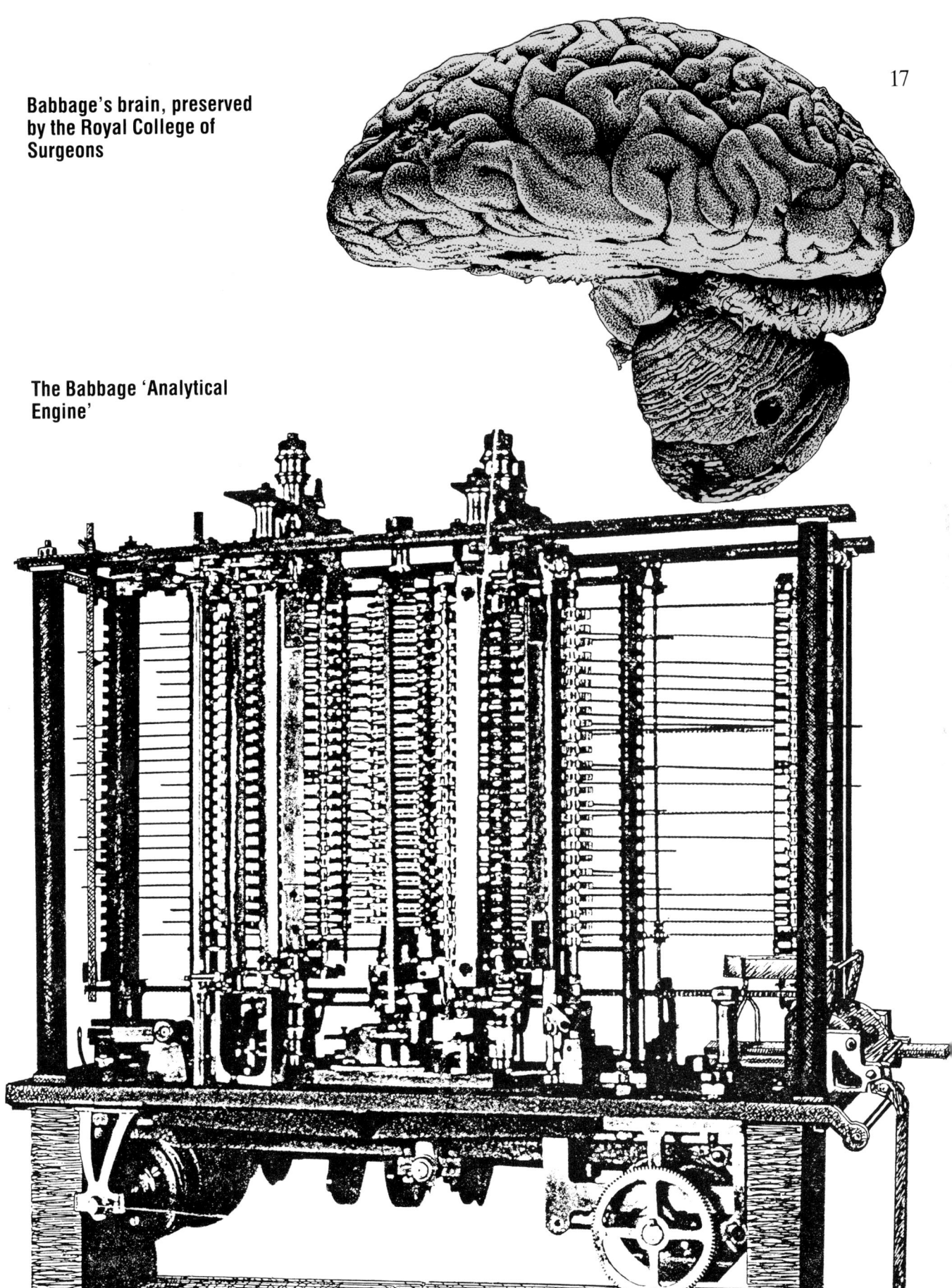

Babbage's brain, preserved
by the Royal College of
Surgeons

The Babbage 'Analytical
Engine'

Sir Henry Bessemer

A section through the converting vessel

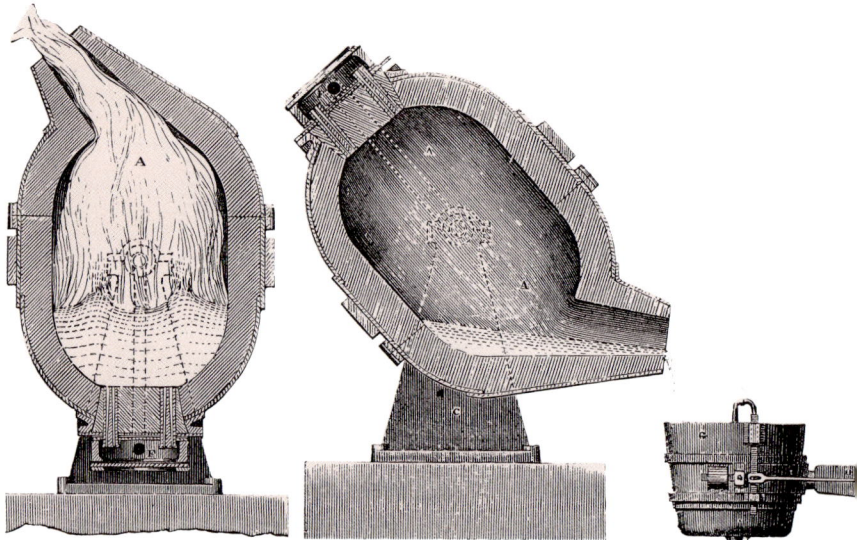

1813
Born 19th January in Charlton, Hertfordshire
1830
Moved to London
1833
Married Ann Allen
1840
Invented 'gold' paint
1856
Announced new process for making steel
1864
Large-scale production of steel under way
1879
Elected a Fellow of the Royal Society; received knighthood
1897
Death of his wife
1898
Died 15th March in London

Although Henry Bessemer is remembered for his process for making cheap steel, that was just one of many inventions. Bessemer was born in 1813. His father was also an engineer and inventor, who ran a thriving business casting type for printers.

When Bessemer was 17 the family moved to London. He spent all his time on inventions, including a machine for setting type. He also proposed a scheme for preventing fraud by perforating documents with official tax stamps, which could not be removed and used again. He was promised a well-paid job as Superintendent of Stamps, but his fiancée, Ann Allen, pointed out that the stamps could be perforated more easily than the documents, so Bessemer's scheme fell through.

Success came when Bessemer discovered how to make cheap 'gold' paint, up to then an expensive import from Germany, from bronze powder. He and his three brothers-in-law set up a factory and

An iron foundry in Wales with two Bessemer converters

made the paint - and a lot of money - for the next 40 years.

Bessemer came to steel production as a result of designing a new artillery shell, which the cast-iron guns of the day were too brittle to fire. He wanted to make steel guns. Steel is made by removing excessive amounts of carbon and other impurities from iron. In the mid-1800s it could be made only in small quantities by heating iron for several days to burn off the carbon, using a great deal of fuel. Bessemer found that blowing air through the molten iron burned the carbon off in about 15 minutes.

Bessemer made a fortune from steel, but one thing in the past rankled: the fact that he had got nothing for the perforated stamp idea. When he raised the matter the Prime Minister, Lord Beaconsfield, offered him the choice of money or a knighthood. Bessemer chose the title because his wife could share it.

Sir Joseph Wilson Swan

Joseph Wilson Swan made important improvements to photography, but he is remembered as one of the two inventors of the electric light bulb, the other being the American, Thomas A. Edison. Swan was born in Sunderland, and was apprenticed to a chemist at the age of 14. When he had completed his training he went to work for a firm in Newcastle which made photographic plates. In those days the plates were used wet; Swan devised a means of making dry plates. He next invented a method of making permanent prints, and in 1879 he patented bromide paper, still used today.

Meanwhile Swan had become interested in the phenomenon of incandescence, in which objects give off light when heated. An American, J. W. Starr, had already produced a form of lamp in which a platinum filament (wire) glowed when an electric current was passed through it in a partial vacuum. Swan experimented with other substances which would stand up to the intense heat produced. In 1860 he made a bulb with a filament of carbonised paper.

Swan was helped in his work by two other developments. One was the invention of the dynamo, which produced a steady supply of electricity. The other was the invention of a pump which could produce an almost complete vacuum. In 1880 he and Edison independently produced workable light bulbs. In 1883 Swan invented a new kind of filament by squeezing nitrocellulose through fine holes to form thread. This invention later led him to make an early form of artificial silk.

1828
Born 31st October in Sunderland
1860
Invented simple electric lamp
1862
Married Frances White
1864
Patented carbon process of photographic printing
1868
Frances Swan died
1871
Married Hannah White; made rapid dry plates
1873
Made first bromide paper
1880
Made workable light bulb
1883
Produced artificial fibres
1904
Received knighthood
1914
Died 27th May in Warlingham Surrey

21

Sir Joseph and Lady Swan in their electrically lighted home

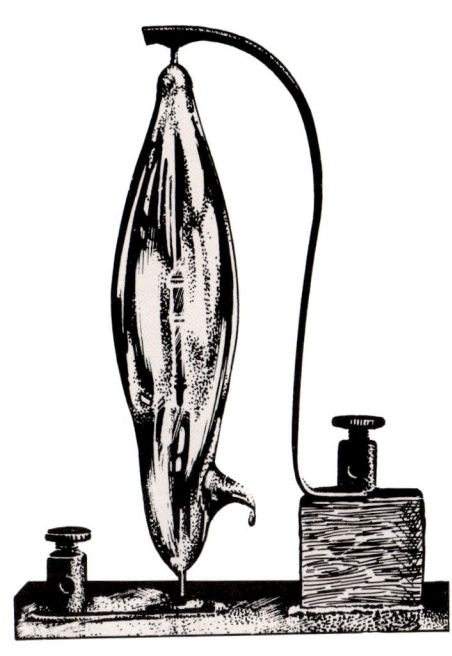

Swan's first incandescent electric lamp

Examples of domestic electric lamps in 1907

John Boyd Dunlop

The pneumatic tyre on which all today's road traffic runs was invented twice, but the first inventor, Robert William Thomson, did little with it. The second bore a name which has become world-famous in connection with tyres: John Boyd Dunlop.

Dunlop was a farmer's son, born in Dreghorn, Ayrshire. He qualified as a veterinary surgeon at the age of 19 and practised for eight years in Edinburgh. In 1867 he moved to Belfast.

Dunlop's nine-year old son John was indirectly responsible for the invention of the pneumatic tyre. Young John had a tricycle, fitted like all cycles of the day with solid rubber tyres. He complained that he was severely shaken as he rode his machine over the irregular granite stones with which the streets of Belfast were paved. Dunlop decided to experiment.

He bought a length of rubber tubing, inflated it and fixed it on to a wooden disc, holding it in place with a strip of canvas. He found it ran along the ground more smoothly than the wheel of his

The Dunlop wire car tyre

The Belfast site of the early experiments

John Dunlop on a bicycle

son's tricycle. Further experiments followed, and Dunlop patented his new tyre in 1888. The following year a racing cyclist on a machine fitted with the new tyres easily defeated riders on machines with solid tyres, and success was assured.

Dunlop and a local businessman, William Harvey Du Cros, formed a company to make tyres for bicycles. The discovery of Thomson's original tyre patent, issued in 1845, meant that Dunlop's patent was not valid, but he had other patents for rims and valves, and the company flourished. Dunlop sold his patent rights and retired to Dublin, where he ran a drapery business.

Four years later the tyre firm was sold for £3,000,000, and the first cars were being fitted with pneumatic tyres. By the time Dunlop died in 1921 nearly 300,000 tons of rubber were being made into tyres every year.

1840
Born 5th February in Dreghorn, Ayrshire
1859
Qualified as a veterinary surgeon in Edinburgh
1867
Married
1867
Moved to Belfast
1887
Invented pneumatic tyre
1888
Received patent for tyre
1889
Pneumatic-tyred bicycle wins race
1890
Production began; Dunlop sold patent rights
1892
Moved to Dublin
1895
First motor-car fitted with pneumatic tyres
1896
Business sold for £3 million
1921
Died 23rd October in Dublin

Experiments with the model wheel

Alexander Graham Bell

Alexander Graham Bell was a teacher of the deaf whose researches into aids for people with hearing problems led him to invent the telephone.

Bell was born in Edinburgh, the son and grandson of teachers of speech correction and elocution. When Bell was 23 his parents emigrated to Canada for their son's health, his two brothers having died of tuberculosis. Bell moved to Boston, Massachusetts, and set up a school for the deaf. Soon after, he became Professor of Vocal Physiology at Boston University.

At the university Bell made many experiments in electrical machines to help the deaf, based on the telegraph. He was assisted by a young mechanic, Thomas Watson. One day Bell was working in one room with Watson listening in another to see if he could make out any sounds like speech transmitted over the electric wires. Suddenly Bell's voice came clearly: 'Mr Watson, come here - I want you!' Bell had spilled acid on his clothes and needed help - but he had also made the first telephone call.

Bell's invention brought him fame and money, and he was able to marry one of his deaf students, Mabel Hubbard. During the rest of his long life Bell continued to work for the deaf and make a series of inventions. They included recording sound on wax discs, making an electric probe for surgery (before the days of X-rays), a form of iron lung, and a hydrofoil craft that reached a speed of 112 km/h (70 mph). He also financed experiments in flight.

He died in 1922 at the summer home - complete with laboratories - which he built on Cape Breton Island, Nova Scotia.

The transmitter-receiver telephone

1847
Born 3rd March in Edinburgh
1864
Became a schoolmaster
1868
Assistant to his father
1870
Emigrated to Canada
1872
Opened school for the deaf in Boston, Massachusetts
1873
Professor of Vocal Physiology at Boston University
1875-1876
Invented the telephone
1877
Married Mabel Hubbard
1878
Moved to Washington, DC
1882
Became US citizen
1885
Built a summer home on Cape Breton Island, Nova Scotia
1890
Founded Association for the Deaf
1898
Became President of the National Geographic Society
1907
Founded the Aerial Experimental Association
1922
Died 2nd August at Cape Breton Island

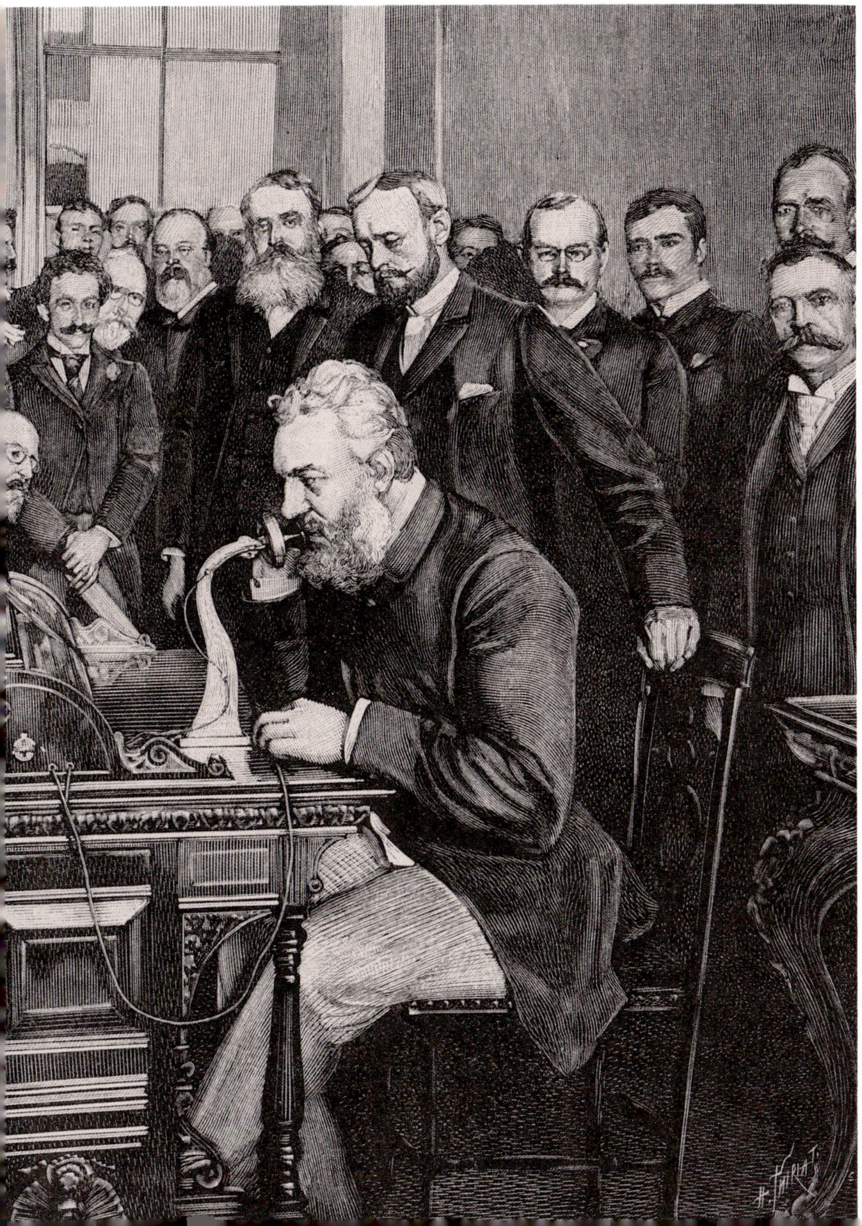

Bell making the first long distance call from New York to Chicago

Sir Ambrose Fleming

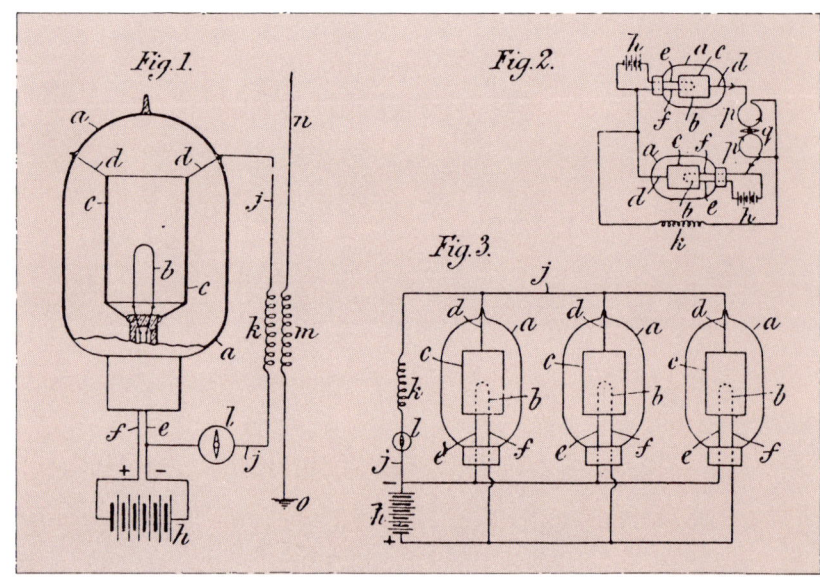

The original patent drawing of the valve

1849
Born 29th November in Lancaster
1870
Graduated from University College, London
1881
Joined Edison Electric Light Company in London·
1885-1926
Professor of Electrical Engineering at University College
1892
Elected as a Fellow of the Royal Society
1896
Began study of 'Edison effect'
1904
Patented thermionic valve
1929
Received knighthood
1933
Married Olive Franks
1945
Died 19th April in Sidmouth, Devon

Radio owed much of its development to the physicist John Ambrose Fleming, who invented the thermionic valve. Fleming's valves were used in radios and all other electronic devices for more than 50 years until the invention of the transistor.

Fleming was born in 1849 in Lancaster, the son of a clergyman. He had a brilliant academic career, winning many honours. He studied at University College, London, the Royal College of Chemistry, and St John's College, Cambridge. For a time he lectured in applied mechanics at Cambridge, then became a consultant to the Edison Electric Light Company in London, helping to develop the countrywide distribution of electricity.

In 1896 the Italian scientist Guglielmo Marconi came to England to develop his new invention - the wireless. Fleming worked with him. One of their problems was to convert the alternating

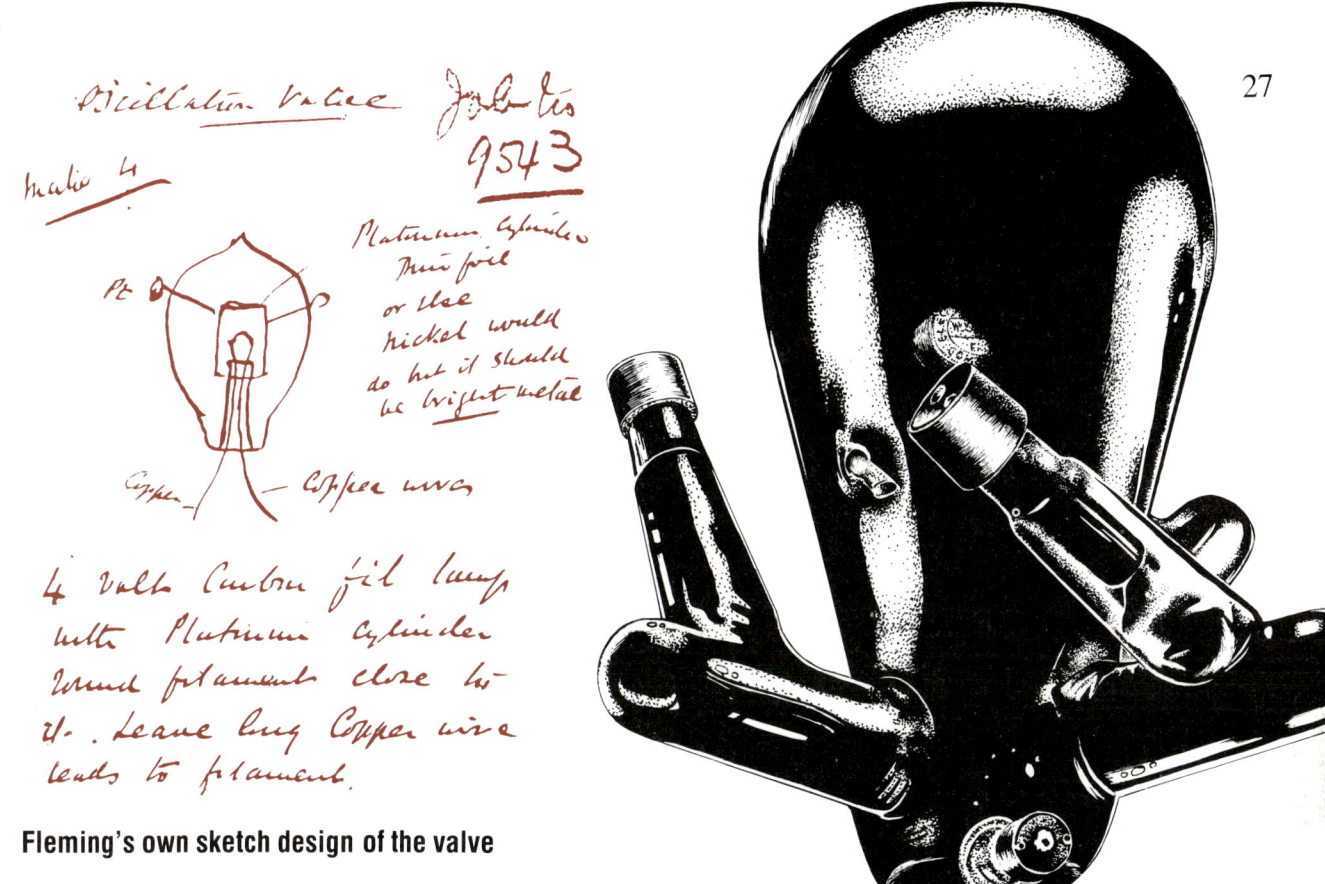

Fleming's own sketch design of the valve

An early Fleming valve

current (which changes the direction of flow many times a second) supplied from the mains into direct current, which was needed for the wireless apparatus.

Fleming began studying an electrical phenomenon known as the 'Edison effect', after the American inventor Thomas Alva Edison, who discovered it. Edison found that if he put a metal plate inside one of his electric light bulbs, next to the filament, and connected it to a positive terminal, current flowed through it. If he connected the plate to a negative terminal, no current flowed. Fleming developed this idea. He called his device a valve because it converted alternating current into direct current.

In between lecturing and teaching, Fleming wrote 17 books and many scientific papers. He was knighted at the age of 80, and married when he was 84. He lived to be nearly 96.

John Logie Baird

The original Baird 'Televisor'

1888
Born 13th August in Helensburgh, Dumbartonshire
1914-1918
Engineer to Clyde Valley Electrical Company
1922
Moved to Hastings
1924
First televised image
1926
First public demonstrations of true television and Noctovision
1927
Sent TV picture by wire from London to Glasgow

John Logie Baird, a Scottish electrical engineer, transmitted the first television picture. Baird was born in Helensburgh, Dumbartonshire, where his father was a Church of Scotland minister. World War I interrupted his electrical engineering studies. Chronic ill-health made him unfit for military service, and he spent the war years as superintendent engineer with an electricity company. Ill-health forced him to give up this work and several business ventures, and he moved to the seaside town of Hastings in East Sussex.

In his attic room in Hastings Baird decided to use his time and what little money he had on research into television. He assembled an apparatus from such unpromising materials as cardboard, scrap timber, needles, and string, and after two years transmitted an image over a

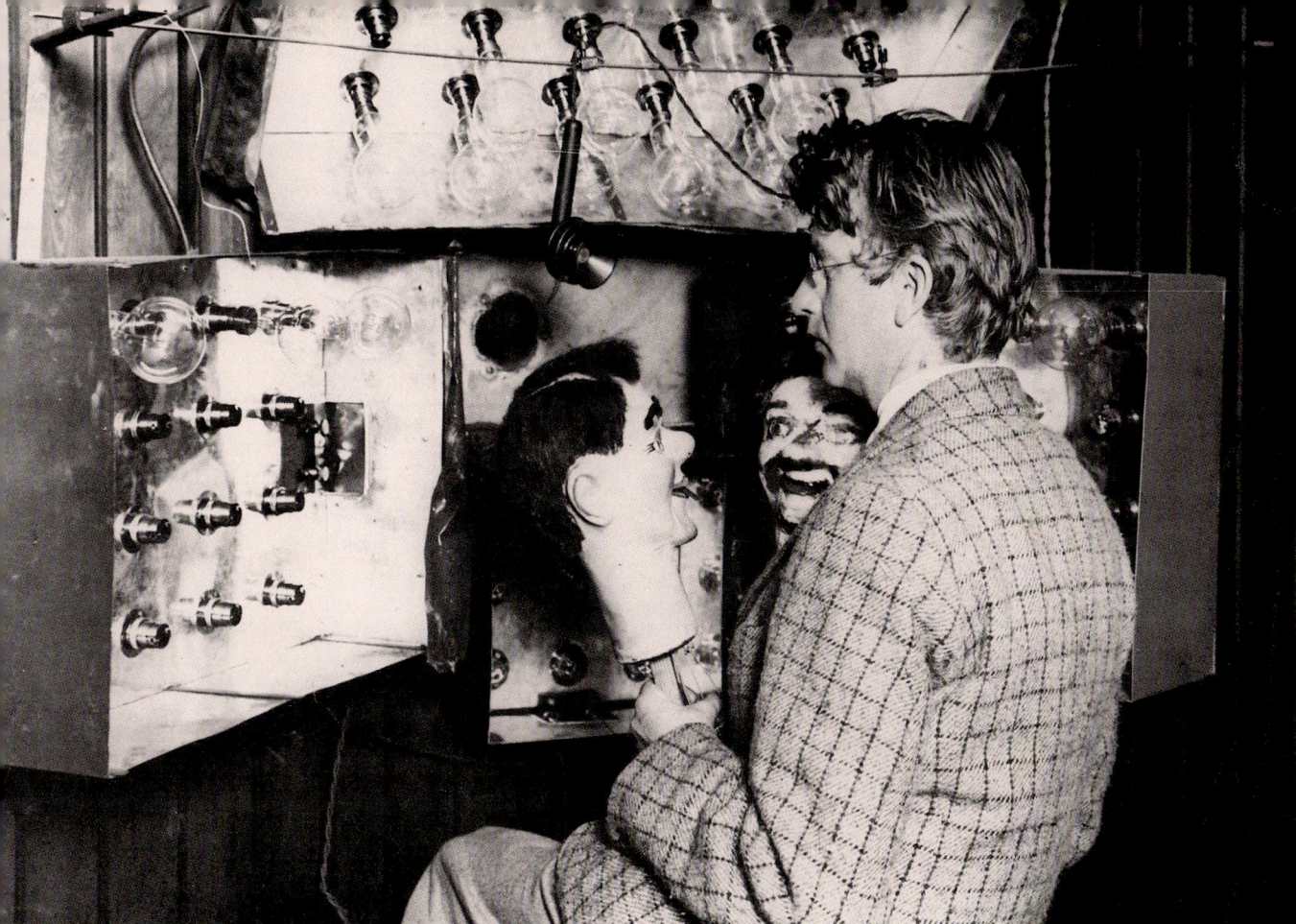

distance of a few feet.

Baird moved to London, and two years and a lot of hard work later he gave the world's first public demonstration of television. The same year he used infra-red rays to 'see' in the dark.

A series of firsts followed: Baird transmitted a picture by wire from London to Glasgow, sent one across the Atlantic to New York, and demonstrated colour, stereoscopic and big-screen TV. The BBC began an experimental service using Baird's mechanical TV system, but dropped it eight years later in favour of a rival electronic system. Baird became technical adviser to Cable and Wireless, and carried on experimental work on colour and stereoscopic TV until his death shortly before his 58th birthday.

1928
First transatlantic TV transmission and first colour TV
1929
BBC and Germans start TV experimental service
1930
Showed big-screen TV
1931
Married Margaret Albu
1937
BBC dropped Baird system
1941
Technical adviser to Cable and Wireless
1946
Died 14th June in Bexhill

'CATSEYE' REG

Percy Shaw

A stray cat inspired Percy Shaw to invent a device that has made motoring safer: the reflecting roadstud, familiarly known as the cat's-eye.

Shaw was born near Halifax, Yorkshire, in 1890. He was the son of a labourer at a dyeworks, who contrived to raise his 14 children on wages of £1 a week. Over the years Shaw built up a road-repairing business and used to drive all over Yorkshire to supervise the work.

One night in 1933 he was driving home in dense fog. In those days there were few road markings to help motorists at night. Shaw recalled : 'It was so dark I couldn't even see the tramlines.' What he did see was the reflection of his car's headlights in the eyes of a cat beside the road.

That cat gave Percy Shaw his great idea: to have reflectors down the middle of the road to guide drivers. It took him months of experimenting to make the first reflecting studs. He had 50 of them installed at his own expense at an accident black-spot, Drighlington crossroads near Bradford. They were a success.

Shaw's stud consists of a cast-iron base which is let into the road surface. The studs are set in a rubber casing in such a way that as a car's wheels go over them the rubber mounting automatically wipes the reflectors, keeping them clear of mud whatever the weather.

Shaw set up a factory to make the studs. They sold slowly at first, but the outbreak of World War II brought the blackout and dimmed headlights, and the studs became essential. They are now used on every major road in Britain, and in other countries.

1890
Born near Halifax, Yorkshire
1933
First idea for cat's-eyes
1934
First 50 roadstuds installed at Drighlington crossroads
1935
Founded Reflecting Roadstuds Ltd
1937-1939
Two-year Transport Ministry test proves worth of Shaw's cat's-eyes
1939-1945
Thousands of cat's-eyes installed to beat blackout
1965
Awarded the OBE
1976
Died 1st September in Halifax

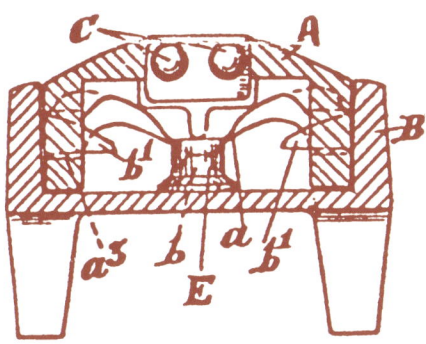

Part of the drawings from the original patent

Percy Shaw with his cat's-eyes

Sir Robert Watson-Watt

1892
Born 13th April in Brechin, Angus
1915
Joined the Meteorological Office
1916
Married Margaret Robertson
1927
Perfected cathode-ray direction-finder
1941
Elected a Fellow of the Royal Society
1942
Knighted, adopted name of Watson-Watt
1952
Marriage dissolved; married Mrs Jean Smith
1964
Death of second wife
1966
Married Dame Katherine Trefusis Forbes
1971
Death of third wife
1973
Died 5th December in Inverness

Robert Alexander Watson-Watt developed radar in Britain and so helped to defeat the German air attacks during World War II. Robert Watt was born in 1892 in Brechin, Angus, where his father, Patrick Watt, was a carpenter. He studied physics and engineering at University College, Dundee, then part of St Andrews University.

In 1915, during World War I, Watt joined the Meteorological Office, where he worked on radio methods of locating thunderstorms. He perfected the idea in 1927, when oscilloscopes (cathode-ray tubes similar to those of TV sets) had become available. Cathode-ray direction-finding (CRDF) was used not only for thunderstorms but for tracking the origin of radio signals.

Eight years later Watt was asked whether it was possible to make a radio death-ray. He replied that it was not, but radio waves could be used to detect the presence and position of an aircraft. He was given the go-ahead to carry on with research into this idea, and soon what later became known as radar (short for **Ra**dio **D**etection **a**nd **R**anging) was being developed and tested.

The success of radar in World War II was due largely to Watt's driving enthusiasm, and his ability to persuade the Air Ministry to adopt all the latest radar improvements. In 1942 he was knighted and adopted the hyphenated surname of Watson-Watt.

After the war Watson-Watt set up a private consultancy, and spent many years in Canada and the United States.

A Lancaster bomber fitted with radar equipment

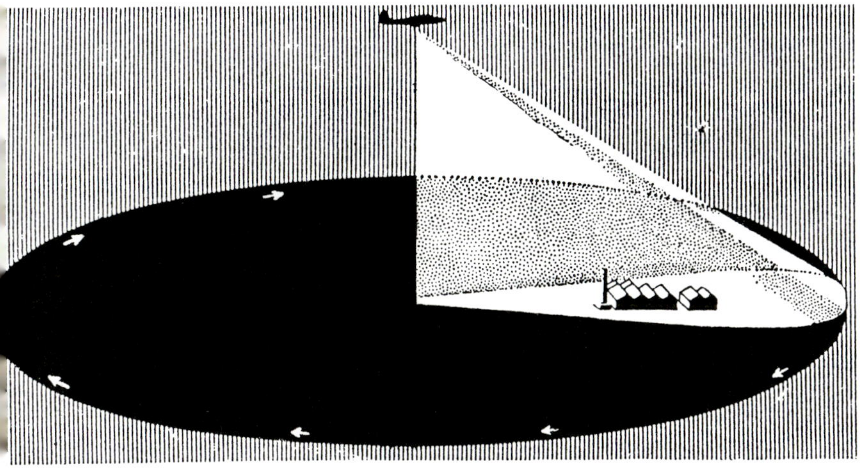

An aircraft 'seeing' at night with radar

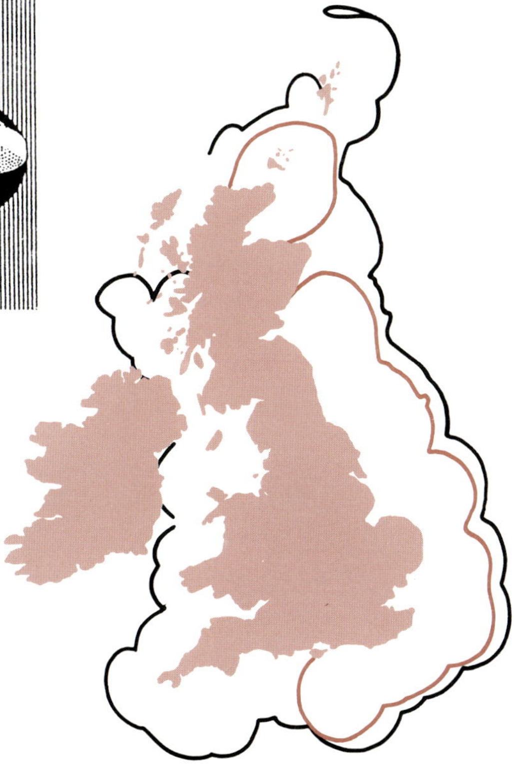

Britain's radar protection at 15,000 feet
1939 ——
1941 ——

Sir Frank Whittle

18 year old RAF apprentice Frank Whittle

1907
Born 1st June in Coventry
1918
Won scholarship to Leamington College
1923
Joined RAF as apprentice
1928
Graduated as pilot officer
1930
Applied for patent on jet engine; married Dorothy Mary Lee
1931
Served as test pilot
1934-1937
At Cambridge University
1937
Completed first experimental jet engine
1941
First flight of Gloster/Whittle E28/39
1944
Gloster Meteor jet fighter went into service

Frank Whittle was one of the pioneers of jet-powered flight. Whittle was born in 1907 in Coventry, where his father was a mechanic and inventor. He joined the Royal Air Force as an apprentice at the age of 16, and qualified as a pilot officer five years later. While training as a pilot he became interested in the possibilities of jet-powered flight, and in 1930 he applied for a patent on a jet engine.

For a time Whittle served as a test pilot, and then the RAF sent him to Cambridge University to take a degree in mechanics. While he was studying he persuaded a firm of bankers to provide the money for Power Jets Limited, a company he formed to develop his jet engine. The first engine was built and tested in 1937. It was far from perfect, but it was sufficiently promising for the Air Ministry to allow Whittle to spend all his

World War Two fighter plane with an early jet engine

time on developing it.

Meanwhile an experimental aeroplane, the Gloster/Whittle E28/39, was being developed to carry the jet engine, and it made its first flight on 15th May, 1941. Further improvements followed, and the Gloster Meteor fighter plane, powered by a Whittle engine, went into service in 1944. It was first used to shoot down German flying bombs.

Whittle retired from the RAF in 1948, and was knighted the same year. The government awarded him £100,000 for his work on the jet engine. During the next few years Whittle held a series of consultancy posts in industry. In 1976 he went to the United States on being appointed a professor at the US Naval Academy at Annapolis, Maryland. Whittle received 50 gold medals, honorary doctorates and other honours.

1947
Elected a Fellow of the Royal Society
1948
Retired from RAF with rank of air-commodore; knighted
1948-1952
Technical adviser to British Overseas Airways Corporation
1952-1957
Adviser to Shell Group
1961-1970
Consultant, Bristol Siddeley Engines/Rolls Royce
1976
Appointed professor at US Naval Academy, Annapolis; first marriage dissolved; married Hazel S. Hall
1986
Received the Order of Merit

How to obtain a patent

The word 'patent' comes from the Latin word meaning 'exposed'. Today it is used to mean the granting of the exclusive right to make, use or sell an invention for a limited period of time. It also gives the patent holder the right to take legal action to protect the invention. In the UK patents are issued by the Patent Office in London and are governed by the 1977 Patents Act. The idea of patenting an invention came from Renaissance Italy, and became popular in England during the reign of Elizabeth I. The first patent law in the UK was established in 1852, and international patents are governed by a convention of 1883. To qualify for a patent an invention must be an improvement or an advancement, although how 'inventive' an invention is can be difficult to decide.

Flowchart of a UK patent application

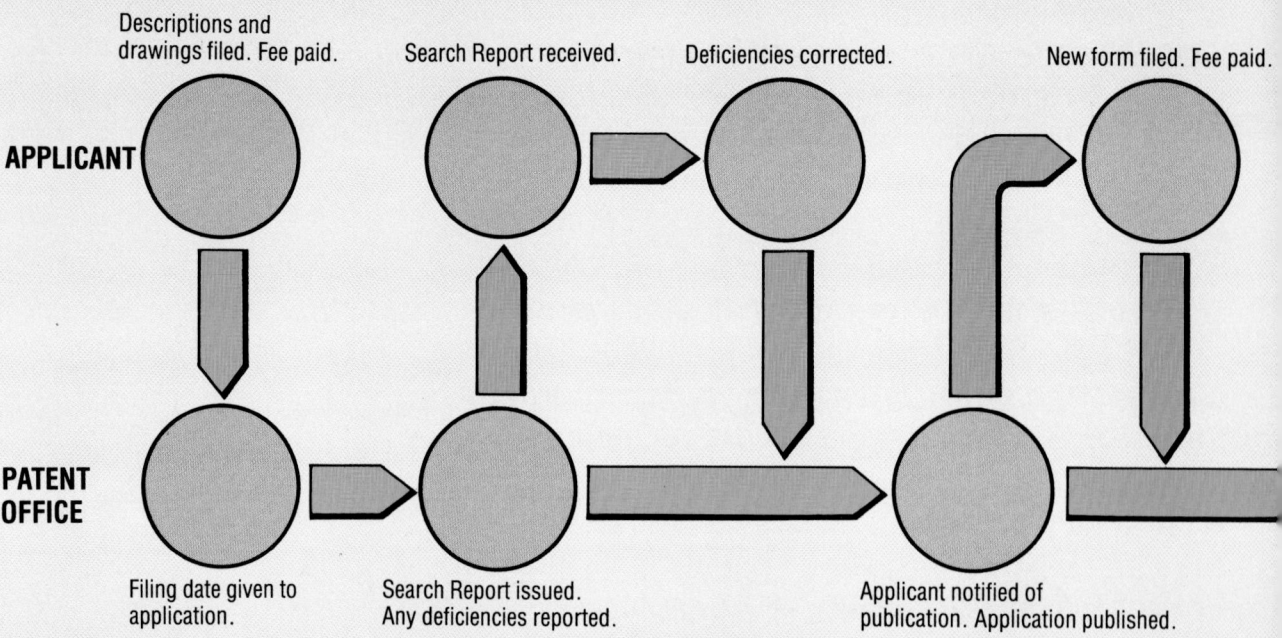

Descriptions and drawings filed. Fee paid.

Search Report received.

Deficiencies corrected.

New form filed. Fee paid.

APPLICANT

PATENT OFFICE

Filing date given to application.

Search Report issued. Any deficiencies reported.

Applicant notified of publication. Application published.

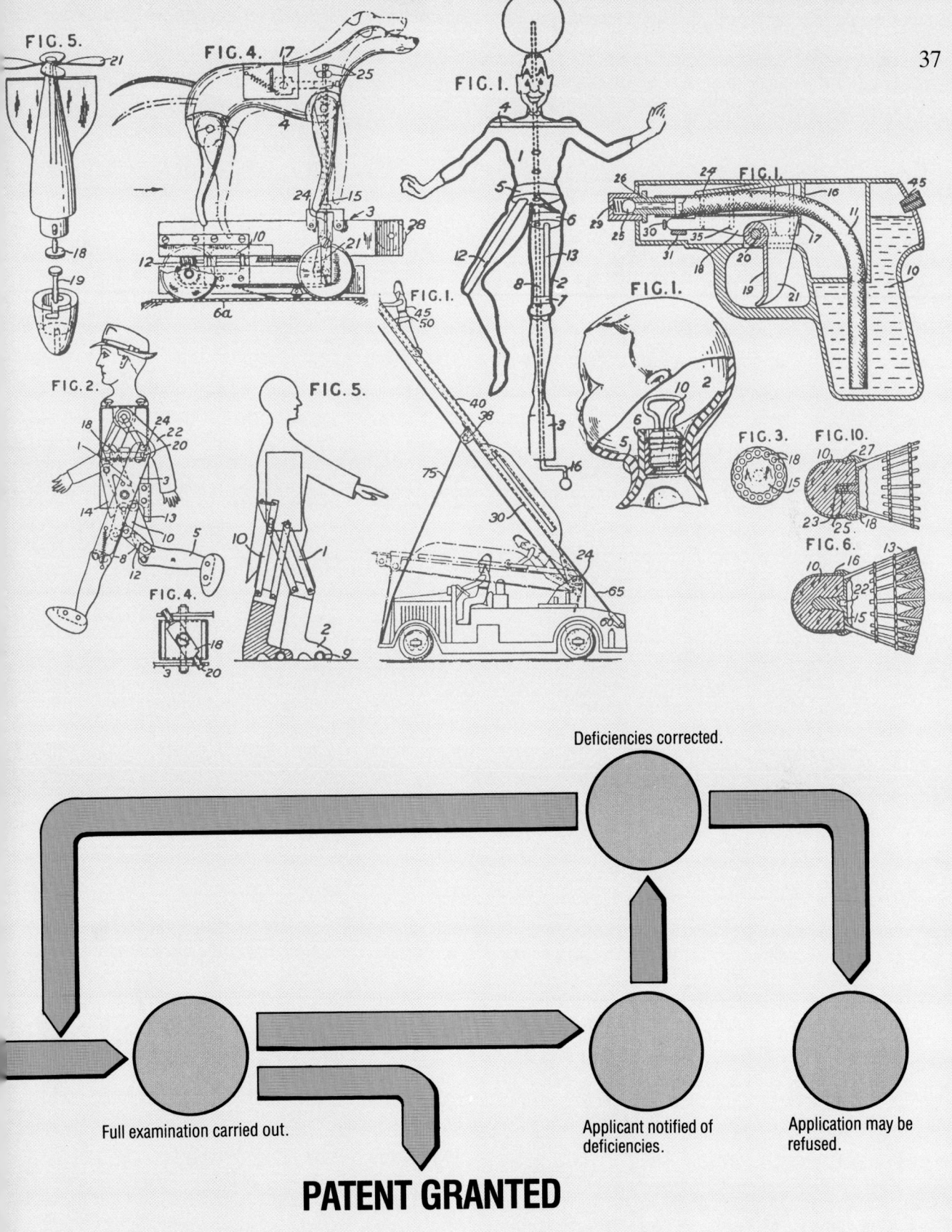

PATENT GRANTED

Deficiencies corrected.

Full examination carried out.

Applicant notified of deficiencies.

Application may be refused.

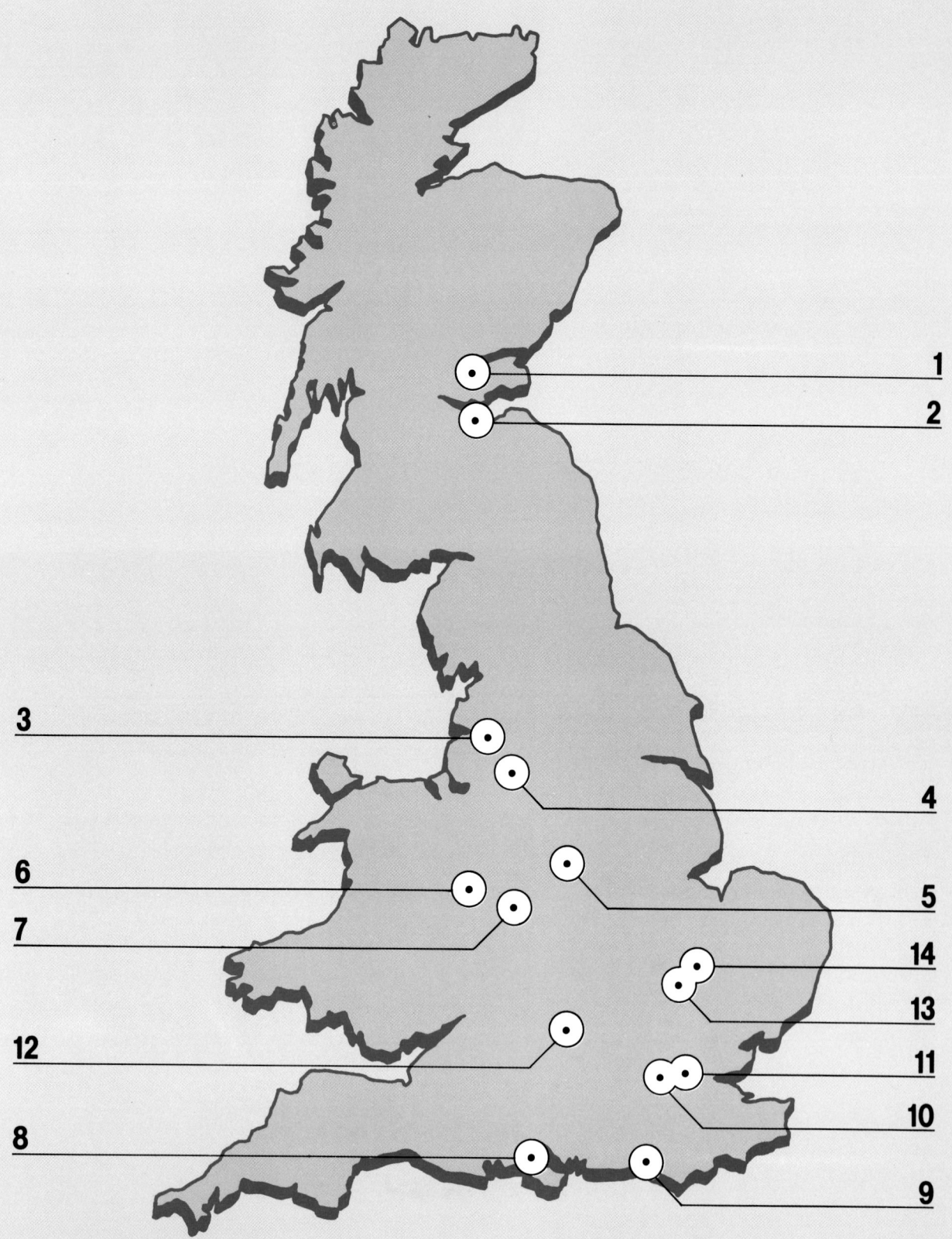

1

2

3

4

5

6

7

14

13

12

11

10

8

9

Museums

1 Strathallan Aircraft Collection, Auchterarder
2 Royal Scottish Museum, Chambers Street, Edinburgh
3 Blackburn Museum, Lewis Textile Collection, Blackburn, Lancashire
   Higher Mill Museum, Helmshore, Lancashire
4 Science Museum, Salford, Lancashire
   Greater Manchester Museum of Science and Industry
5 Derby Industrial Museum, The Silk Mill, Off Full Street, Derby
6 Ironbridge Gorge Open Air Museum, Ironbridge, Nr. Telford, Shropshire
7 Birmingham Museum of Science and Technology, Newhall Street, Birmingham
8 National Motor Museum, Palace House, Beaulieu, Hampshire
9 British Engineering, Nevill Road, Hove, Sussex
10 BL Heritage Display, Syon Park, Brentford, Middlesex
11 National Maritime Museum, Greenwich
   Science Museum, Exhibition Road, London SW7
   Telecom Technology Showcase, Victoria Street, London EC4
   IBA's Broadcasting Gallery, Brompton Road, London SW3
12 Museum of the History of Science, Oxford
13 Shuttleworth Collection of Historic Aeroplanes, Cars and Bicycles, Old Warden Aerodrome, Biggleswade, Old Warden, Bedfordshire
14 Whipple Museum of the History of Science, Cambridge
   Imperial War Museum, Duxford Airfield, Nr. Cambridge

Useful addresses

British Association for the Advancement of Science
Youth Activities
Fortress House,
23 Savile Row,
London W1X 1AB

The British Technology Group
101 Newington Causeway
London SE1 6BU

Chartered Institute of Patent Agents
Staple Inn Buildings,
London WC1V 7PZ

The Engineering Council
10 Maltravers Street
London WC2R 3ER

The Institute of Inventors
19 Fosse Way
Ealing
London W13 0BZ

Institute of Patentees and Inventors
Staple Inn Buildings South
355 High Holborn
London WC1 7PX

The Patent Office
State House
66/71 High Holborn
London WC1R 4TP

Society of Industrial Artists and Designers
Nash House
12 Carlton House Terrace
London SW1Y 5AH

Index

SCIENTISTS

BACON

BOYLE

NEWTON

HALLEY

THE HERSCHELS

JENNER

DALTON

FARADAY

DARWIN

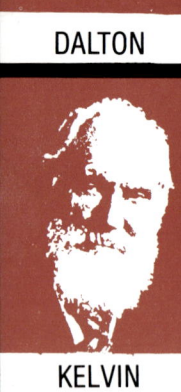

KELVIN

LISTER

MAXWELL

THOMSON

FLEMING

CRICK

EXPLORERS

FROBISHER

HUDSON

COOK

PARK

FRANKLIN

STURT

ROSS

LIVINGSTONE

SPEKE

STANLEY

YOUNGHUSBAND

SCOTT

SHACKLETON

FUCHS

FIENNES